Wickiup

Written by
Kevin M. Mitchell

Illustrated by
Kimberly L. Dawson Kurnizki

The Rourke Book Company, Inc.
Vero Beach, Florida 32964

Printed in the United States of America

2

Library of Congress Cataloging-in-Publication Data

Mitchell, Kevin M., 1962-
    Wickiup / Kevin M. Mitchell.
        p. cm. — (Native American homes)
    Includes bibliographical references and index.
    ISBN 1-55916-276-7
    1. Wickiups—Juvenile literature. 2. Indians of North America—Dwellings—Juvenile literature. 3. Indians of North America—Dwellings—Great Basin—Juvenile literature. 4. Indians of North America—Material culture—Great Basin—Juvenile literature. [1. Wickiups. 2. Indians of North America—Great Basin. 3. Indians of North America—Dwellings.] I. Title. II. Series.

E98.D9 M57 2000
979004'97—dc21
                                                    00-036928

Contents

The Great Basin

The area called the Great Basin covers a big part of the western United States. It includes Utah, Nevada, and most of western Colorado and southern Idaho. Smaller parts of New Mexico, California, and other states are also included.

The *basin* lies between two large mountain ranges, the Wasatch Mountains of Utah and the Sierra Nevada of California. The Great Basin is actually not one large basin but many smaller ones. They are separated by smaller mountain ranges that run north and south.

The weather is very hot most of the year. In winter, winds sweeping down from the Northwest create short periods of cold weather. The land has little rainfall. Much of the Great Basin is nearly as hot and dry as a desert. However, there are more plants there than in a real desert. In fact, the Great Basin contains a rich variety of plants and animals.

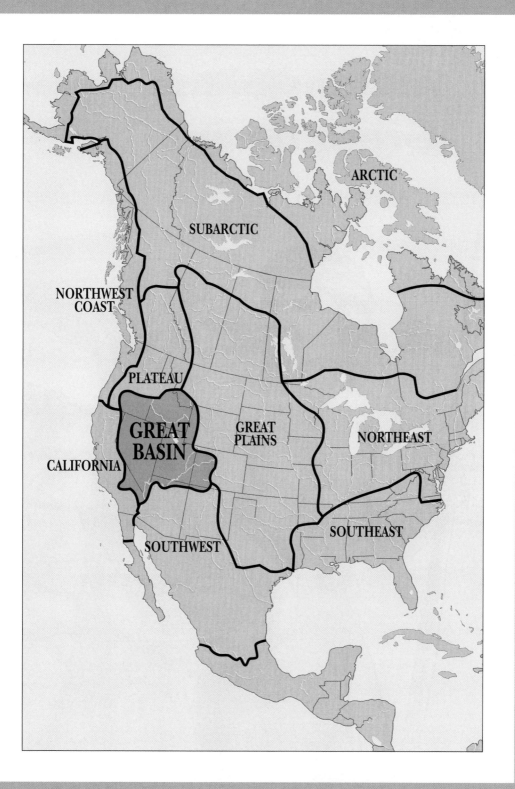

ARCTIC

SUBARCTIC

NORTHWEST
COAST

PLATEAU

GREAT
BASIN

GREAT
PLAINS

NORTHEAST

CALIFORNIA

SOUTHWEST

SOUTHEAST

Indians of the Great Basin

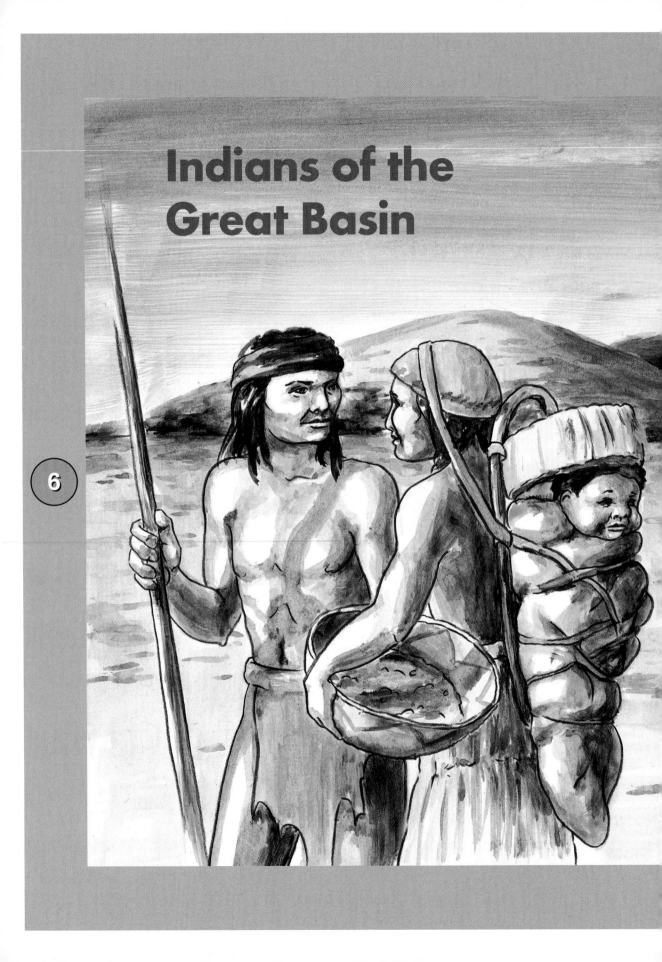

The Indians who roamed the Great Basin lived there for many thousands of years. Some of the main Great Basin tribes are the Utes, Paiutes, Shoshones, Bannocks, and Washoes. In the past these groups were *nomads* who did little farming.

The Great Basin tribes mostly lived in smaller groups called bands. A band was made up of a number of local groups that traveled and camped in the same general area. They would work together as a large family. Religion was part of the people's everyday life. They performed *rituals* to ask the spirits for help with hunting, and they gave blessings with every new home they built.

The Basin Indians obtained horses from the Spanish, who came to the Americas in the sixteenth century. Horses gave them the ability to travel faster and farther.

Great Basin tribes such as the Paiutes and Washoes were famous for making strong and beautiful baskets. They used baskets for everything from carrying water to cooking food.

The Wickiup

Wickiups were the Great Basin tribes' main type of housing, but the people used them for only part of the year. Wickiups could be built quickly. They were ideal for Indians who did not need permanent homes.

Grass or leaves were layered around the frame of poles.

A wickiup was usually dome-shaped. It had a frame of willow or oak poles. The frame would be covered with grass, brush, or bark. Sometimes a wickiup would not even have a door. Some wickiups were big, but most were made for four or fewer people. Buffalo hide was used to cover the wickiup in winter. In winter a wickiup also had a *firepit* and a smoke hole.

Occasionally the wickiup would be picked up and moved with the Indian band. It could be placed on its side and pulled by horse. Usually, however, Indians would leave wickiups behind, never to return to them.

Building the Wickiup

Selecting a good spot was the first step in building a wickiup. The Indians would select a level and well-drained site. They then dug a shallow trench about 12 feet (3.6 meters) in diameter.

The next step was finding good wood for the frame. The wood needed to be strong yet bendable. Willow or oak poles were ideal. Once the Indians found good wood poles, they cut off the branches and leaves. Sometimes they had to whittle the wood down to make the poles thin enough to bend.

Then they planted the poles in a circle. The poles were bent toward the center and tied together at the top. The outer wickiup frame was about 8 feet (2.4 meters) across.

The frame was the first part to be built.

11

Sometimes tough *tamarisk* saplings would be used for the frame. Tamarisk is a thick, sturdy desert shrub. A wickiup built with tamarisk could be as high as 7 feet (2 meters) at the center. After the frame was built, a covering was needed. The type of covering used depended on what was available and what time of year it was.

In the hot seasons, the covering would usually be *yucca* leaves and grasses. The Indians held the covering together by layering the leaves and grass around the poles. Pieces of cottonwood, oak, or sumac might be tied to the peak. The leaves and branches were left on.

Sometimes, especially in the rainy season, strips of tree bark were used in covering the wickiup. Tree bark is stronger and more durable when it is wet, and it is less likely to break and crumble than when dry. In cold weather, buffalo skin would be put over the wickiup for extra warmth.

After constructing a wickiup, the builders would say a prayer. The Indians of the Great Basin were very spiritual, and they would ask their gods for blessings. There usually was not one person who was the spiritual leader in the group. All members would contribute to the ritual—the important final step in the building of a wickiup.

The Wickiup Door and Firepit

For most of the year, Indians used wickiups only for sleeping and for shelter from the sun. Yet no matter where in the Great Basin the Indians lived, the winter would be rainy or cold for at least a short time. Then doors and indoor firepits were needed.

Doors were made from buffalo hide or from small, thin logs. For hide doors, the buffalo skin was stretched and prepared so that it would stay tough enough to protect the inside of the wickiup from bad weather. Doorways always faced east, toward the morning's rising sun.

Firepits were needed inside for cooking and warmth. If the ground was not too hard, the Indians would dig a small hole for the fire. The hole was always placed in the center of the wickiup. Directly above would be a smoke hole so people could cook and stay warm without breathing too much smoke.

The Appearance of the Wickiup

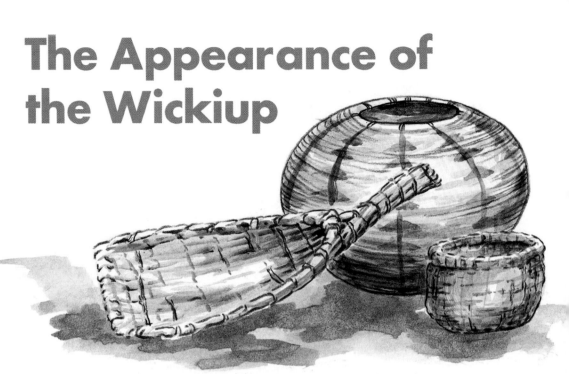

The people of the Great Basin who lived in wickiups followed animal herds for hunting. They also moved to different areas looking for food such as berries and piñon nuts. Since their homes were temporary, they did not spend much time decorating them.

Gathering food, hunting, and raising their families were more important to the people than decorating something that would soon be left behind. The winter covering of buffalo or deer hide was the only part that the Indians carried with them to their next stop. Sometimes they did paint the hide covers.

The Indians who lived in wickiups did not paint much. They did not make pottery, either, like many other Indians, but they took great pride in their basket-weaving. Even their boats and houses were built like baskets. The wickiup has been described as a big upside-down basket.

A wickiup with a ramada, or shade house.

Ramadas and Lean-Tos

There is little shade in many parts of the Great Basin, and it gets very hot in the summer. The temperature is often above 100 degrees Fahrenheit (38 degrees Celsius). The people needed shelter from the sun so they could do their work and relax in comfort.

Ramadas, or "shade houses," are even simpler than wickiups. Four upright poles support a roof of brush. Sometimes a ramada has one wall. Ramadas provide a cool, shaded area, and Great Basin Indians still use them today.

When the Indians of the Great Basin camped in hilly areas, they sometimes built lean-tos. A lean-to is a type of wickiup that uses a hill as part of its construction. The Indians would place poles and brush in wickiup fashion, but the structure would also be supported by the hill. The people used this type of housing when they were staying somewhere for a very short time.

Wickiup Villages

The Indians of the Great Basin traveled in small groups. They did not follow a chief, as Indians in much of North America did. One man in the group was designated a leader, sometimes called a "talker." He would look for good places to camp. Once a spot was chosen, an instant wickiup village would be built.

Eight to fifteen wickiups would be built, and they could all be built in a day. Since there was plenty of land, there would be lots of space between each wickiup. The Indians built them in all sizes. Single men needed only enough space to lie down, but families needed more room.

Great Basin Indians usually built wickiup villages in areas that had little vegetation. Often they were built at the foot of a mountain. Usually one or two ramadas were also built in the center of the camp. They provided shade for the women and children while the men went to hunt.

Living in a Wickiup

The inside of the wickiup was dark during the daytime. No light came through the covering of grass, bark, and *thatch*. Some light came in through the door. If the wickiup had a smoke hole, a little light would also come in from above. There was not enough light to do work, however.

The darkness of the inside did not matter very much. People stayed inside during the day only when the weather was unusually cold or rainy. For most of the year, very little rain falls in the Great Basin.

Most wickiups were just tall enough for a person to stand up in the middle, but they were too small to allow much moving around. Work, meeting, socializing, and eating were almost always done outside. Wickiups were used almost entirely for sleeping.

Longer wickiups were built if the people intended to stay in one place for a while.

When members of a band were sure they would be staying longer than usual in a certain area, they sometimes built larger wickiups. These were built almost the same way as smaller ones, but they were longer. Part of the covering was made of logs. Larger families used these wickiups, and more indoor activities would take place.

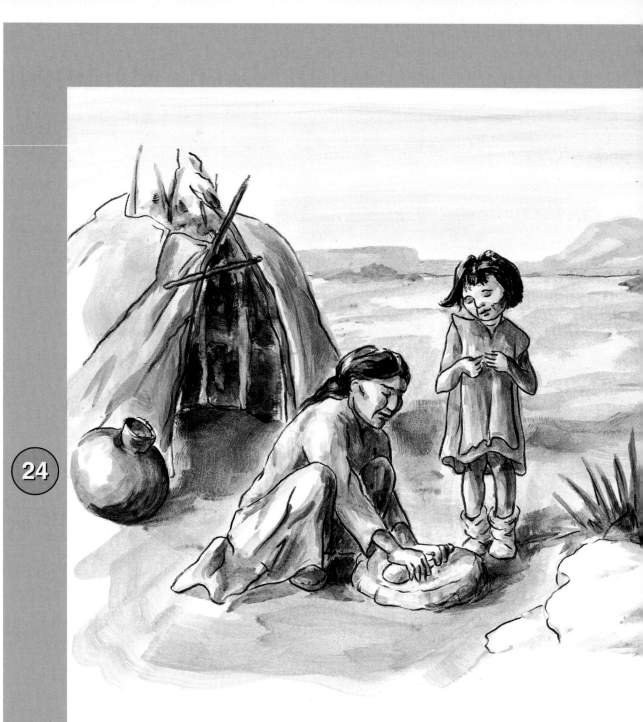

The family's sleeping area was covered with animal furs. Tools and clothing were kept by the walls. Women prepared food close to the center of the wickiup, near the firepit.

Late in the nineteenth century, wickiups changed. The Great Basin Indians did not roam as much as much as they used to. They began to wrap canvas cloth around the side of the wickiup that faced the harsh winds. Wire or cloth strips replaced the branches and yucca strips on the outside. Wooden doors were used more often. The people began putting hinges on the doors and even attached padlocks to protect their belongings.

Wickiups Today

No Indians live in wickiups any more. Since the 1860's, Indians of the Great Basin have mostly lived on *reservations*. When they started settling in one place, they needed permanent homes. The religion and storytelling traditions of the people were more important to them than their types of homes. They preserved these traditions more carefully than their grass huts.

The ramada is still used today. The Indians of the Great Basin still need protection from the hot sun. Ramadas are even more important now than they were when they were first being built centuries ago. Now they are seen as places to gather and visit. They are also a connection to the traditions of the past.

In 1986, President Ronald Reagan declared 77,100 acres (31,200 hectares) of the Great Basin a *national park*. People enjoy camping there much as the Indians did many years ago.

Make a Model Wickiup

What you will need:

round plastic container that held margarine
   or whipped cream
twigs or small sticks
leaves and dry grass
glue
scissors

To make your wickiup:

1. Work with the open top of the plastic container facing down. Cut a small, rounded doorway. Cut it so that it goes about three-quarters of the way up.

2. Cut a small hole in the center of the top of the container for the smoke hole.

3. Glue sticks and twigs all around the outside of the container. They should go side-to-side rather than up-and-down.

4. Apply another coat of glue if necessary and cover the glue and sticks completely with leaves. Do not cover the doorway or the smoke hole, but cover the rest of the shell so that no plastic is showing.

Glossary

basin: an area that is enclosed or partly enclosed and that has a surface lower than the areas around it.

firepit: a small hole in which fires are built.

national park: an area of land set aside by the government for preservation and protection from development.

nomads: people who wander from place to place and do not have a permanent home.

reservation: a piece of land set aside for use only by Native Americans.

ritual: the form and actions of a ceremony or celebration; often religious in nature.

tamarisk: a tall, thick shrub found in hot, dry places; has tiny leaves and masses of flowers.

thatch: plant material such as straw used to cover a house.

yucca: a plant in the lily family that has large, rigid leaves and woodlike stems.

Further Reading

Carter, Alden R. *The Shoshoni.* New York: Franklin Watts, 1989.

Flanagan, Alice K. *The Utes.* New York: Children's Press, 1998.

Fradin, Dennis B. *The Shoshone.* Chicago: Childrens Press, 1992.

Joseph, Alvin M. *Indian Heritage of America.* New York: Houghton Mifflin, 1991.

Monroe, Jean Guard, and Ray A. Williamson. *First Houses: Native American Homes and Sacred Structures.* Boston: Houghton Mifflin, 1993.

31

Suggested Web Sites

Native American Desert Peoples (tribes)
<www.desertusa.com/ind1/du_peo_ute.html>
<www.desertusa.com/ind1/du_peo_paiute.html>
Native America (native lore; animal totems)
<www2.itexas.net/~sparrow/native.htm>
The People (historical photos)
<dmla.clan.lib.nv.us/docs/museums/reno/expeople/people.htm>

Index

Photo credits: Cover, pp. 9, 20-21, Marilyn "Angel" Wynn; p.11, Eda Rogers; pp. 19, 23, Dan Polin.